THE TALES END

A Selection of Short Stories

Written and Compiled

By

Judi Waller

Copyright 2021 Judi Waller

Copyright Desert Quest - 1997 Craig Springsteen

Copyright My Life So Far – Rochelle Springsteen undated

Front cover designed by Joseph Fay from Disruptive Publishing

Graphics By David Wicks

Photographs reproduced by permission of Waller / Springsteen Families

Published By Disruptive Publishing

Edited By Sharon Hawthorne

All rights reserved. No part of this publication may be reproduced, stored in a retrieval system or transmitted in any form or by any means (electronic, mechanical, photocopying, recording or by any process now known or in the future) without written permission of the author or artist. Brief quotations that are credited to the publication and the author are permitted.

ISBN# 978-0-6452352-2-7 print

ISBN# 978-0-6455278-1-0 ebook

Acknowledgements

The Antigonish Poem by William Hughes Mearns

Other Poems by Bert Russell (a departed friend)

Illustrations by David Wicks - DMW Photo graphics

"As I was going up the stair,

I met a man who wasn't there!

He wasn't there again today,

Oh, how I wish he'd go away!"

                      The Antigonish by William Hughes Mearns   1922

                                  (Poem originated in 1899)

Table of Contents

PRELUDE 9
BELLS! 11
MY IMMIGRATION JOURNEY 13
THE PARK BENCH 19
ANNIE'S MAN 25
MEETING A VIKING: A LOVE STORY 27
LONG AWAITED TRIP TO LONGREACH 37
THE SAILOR 47
THE JUNKET OF THE SAILING VESSEL 49
A LEAP OF FAITH 83
THE HUNGRY SEA 87
THE ANTIGONISH 91
WALKS ON HIS TOES! 93
THE DESERT QUEST 99
MY LIFE SO FAR... 103
ABOUT THE AUTHOR 107

PRELUDE

Many years ago, I tried my hand at writing poetry, to no avail. But I have a few small writings from friends, my dear granddaughter Rochelle and the ilk which I will include under their guidance and permission, plus a short story from my dear departed Grandson.

I have for many years wanted to be a writer but never had the courage. I was always good at story telling in my school days - writing essays, what a shame I did not keep some of them. What comes out of the minds of young children can be much better than when one becomes an adult.

The stories to follow are generally of my own thoughts and experiences.

Some ten or so years ago we lived in a place called Maryborough, three hours north of Brisbane. We had a very old home there, built in 1873, a Gentleman's Residence they say. The name of the home was 'Rosedale'. The walls were a foot thick with an abortion of a veranda built over the front door, the result of which took away any character the home had when observing the house from the street. We spent nine years in Maryborough, during this time we completely renovated this lovely old cottage, which incidentally did have a resident ghost, however that is another story to be told at a later date.

Across from the home on the other side of the street lived an elderly gentleman, name of Bert Russell. Now, Bert was a poet and before moving away - to coin a phrase Bert went bush - but before he did, he gave me several poems which I have included within these pages, please enjoy.

Bert has since gone to a higher authority. "Rest in Peace," my Friend! Below are the first two verses of Bells by Bert Russell 20/9/00

BELLS!

When we were young and marched to school

with pencil, book and slate,

They made sure we had no excuse if ever we were late,

The school went in at half past nine in rain hail or shine,

At quarter past a bell was rung to get us there on time.

The chapel bells chime merrily to announce the newly wed,

But the same bells toll solemnly when heralding the dead,

For the bell can be melodious or it can lonely ring,

The circumstance determines whether we cry or sing.

                                        by Bert Russell 20/9/00

MY IMMIGRATION JOURNEY

The reason for leaving our homeland was for a better life after the war in Europe and to see our Uncle John Henry, whom we (that is me, my sister Ann and brother John) had never met. Uncle John had seven children and they all lived in a little place called Davistown, near Gosford, on the north coast of NSW.

We arrived at the Southampton docks at 3.30pm, passed through customs fairly quickly and completed all formalities. The organisation was good. Embarked aboard H.M.T 'Asturias' at 4.00pm. (The Asturias was used as a troop ship during the war then converted to a migrant ship). We cast off and commenced our 12,000 mile journey to Australia. 7.00pm had dinner, all very tired. During the evening with the light fading, we passed the Needles on our Southern Quarter. As a migrant ship, male and female where segregated. Turned in, Dad and brother John on E deck, John berth No. 1012 and Dad No.1013. Mum, Ann and myself were on C deck, Mum berth 183, Ann 185 and myself 187. The date was November the 2nd 1949.

We kept busy throughout the trip playing deck tennis and various other types of entertainment. We passed Cape de Roca, the most westerly point of Europe at 4.15pm on the 4th of November.

Nov. 5th, we ran down the coast of Spain - the ranges and mountains shrouded in mist. We passed the Australian Emigrant Ship, 'Empire Parent', homeward bound.

Nov. 6th, Sunday, clocks were put forward a half hour.

Nov. 7th, we sight the coast of Malta.

Nov. 8th, it was blowing hard and the clocks went forward again 30 mins.

Nov. 9th, sixty miles offshore, couldn't see much, clear sky and blue sea. 4.55pm, take on a pilot and altered course for Port Said. 5.30pm passed the statue to the Frenchman who built the Suez Canal. (Ferdinand de Lesseps in 1854 was the French Consul to Cairo under an agreement with the Ottoman Government of Egypt). Many wrecks were visible in the approaches - the aftermath of the war.

When it became dark, we tied to a Buoy in Port Said Harbour. There were small craft everywhere, absolute bedlam all shouting and trying to sell goods - the bargaining continued until after midnight.

Nov 10th, we were underway again and heading for Canal. Deserts as far as the eye could see stretched all around. Saw a caravan of Camels.

Nov.11th, East of Suez and in the Red Sea.

Nov.12th, ran through two storms.

Nov. 13th, passed a few islands blowing hard. 12 midnight dropped Anchor in Aden Harbour.

Nov.14th, went ashore in Aden, hired a taxi and drove out to the Oasis and gardens, past the salt flats with their windmills built by Italians. Saw much damage where the buildings and schools of the Jews had been destroyed by the Arabs. The town of Aden appears to have been built in an extinct volcano. On return to the ship I, and a bunch of other youngsters, swam in Aden Harbour. Had we been older we may never have done it - what a filthy harbour, but the young don't see. (What it is? They believe, they are invincible).

Nov.15th, we were 4,923 miles from Southampton.

Nov.16th, well into the Arabian Sea.

Nov. 17th, ran steadily across the Arabian sea. The flying fish watched from the bow were most interesting.

Nov.18th and Nov.19th, there were quite a number of fishing craft around 11am. Anchor in Colombo Harbour. I loved Colombo, we went ashore and had a swim in the baths at the Galle Face Hotel, then spent some time going through the Moonstone Mines. What a lovely place.

Nov. 20th, the Indian Ocean.

Nov. 21st, crossed the equator. Weather good, fine, somewhat hot. There where celebrations with King Neptune on crossing the equator.

Nov. 22nd, weather was hot and some squalls.

Nov. 23rd, passed Cocos islands, morning was warm and sunny.

Nov. 24th, it was much cooler.

Nov. 25th, it blew hard and was quite chilly.

Nov. 26th, it was still blowing and seas were rough.

Nov. 27th, Dad was called out to assist with a flooded cabin, the result of which is not now in my memory and not written in the daily diary. We approached Fremantle.

Nov. 28th, ran down the Australian coast.

Nov. 29th, started to cross the Great Australian Bight.

Nov.30th, clocks went on another 30 minutes, we had been doing this all the way.

Dec.1st, it was cold and overcast, 2.00pm abeam Cape Nelson.

Dec. 2nd, we docked alongside in Melbourne .

Dec. 3rd, cast off and headed for Sydney.

Dec.4th, set a course for Sydney. 4.30pm abeam of Montague Island.

Dec. 5th, 1949, My family: Norman Ronald (Mac) McNicol, his wife Noreen (Henry) McNicol and children Ann Veronica McNicol, Judith Mary McNicol and John Henry McNicol arrived in Australia and travelled to Davistown, near Gosford in New South Wales, to start a new life.

Impressions on our arrival! On the whole pretty good, and for us youngsters a whole new adventure, though we were all split up for some time until we were able to obtain a home - which we eventually did in Maroubra NSW. From then on things improved dramatically, it is after all what one makes of the changes and the willingness to compromise.

There was a great deal of compromises to start off with. We stayed in the guest house in Davistown for a short while. There was a small house in the grounds of the guest house, which had been used to house chickens, this was offered to Mum and Dad as a means of accommodation. So, my mother spent the first couple of weeks on her hands and knees cleaning this disgusting little place to make it habitable for us to live in. She did this with tears running down her face, but she never gave up and we moved in.

I then went down to Sydney and my first job was as a telephonist for Samson's school of music. My sister secured some digs at Manly and also a job in Sydney town. I also got digs in Manly. Dad went to work in Bankstown at an aircraft company and commuted to Davistown. Mum remained in the chicken run. Our brother went to school in Gosford.

Thus was the start of our lives in Australia

THE PARK BENCH

A short road with a 'No Through' sign at the beginning and hardly a street light to be seen.

At the end there is a park, well-manicured grounds, lawns like a bowling green. It rises up a gentle slope and drops softly on the other side, giving a wide expanse of rural greenery, soft meadows and farmhouses in the distance.

Off to one side one can see a rather large manor house, at one time used as an orphanage, now a very respectable school for boys. A very peaceful scene and nestling against the side, just as the rise drops away, is a dilapidated park bench made of timber and iron sides. There had been some attempt to tidy it up with fresh paint, most probably by someone living nearby rather than a council project, but one could see that it had seen better days.

Rosa always went there and had done for years. Her old Grandmother had lived in the street and, when Rosa's mother had passed into the almighty, as Gran always said, Rosa had gone to live with her grandmother. Once she had discovered the park bench and the lovely place it had become, Rosa would run up the hill every day, hail, rain or shine, to sit and contemplate the view. Such peace and quiet, such wonderment.

It was there, so much happened to change her life. It was there she met Jack. Jack was a boy from the school, a live-in student, tall, blond with a lopsided grin and a funny way of holding his head to one side, seriously quiet yet full of fun. He used to sneak out, come up the hill and sit on the bench beside her. They did not speak much at first, but as time progressed they started to talk and tell each other about their lives, laughing at each other's experiences. The years progressed. Jack left the school and started work on one of the neighbouring farms. He was quite clever and never afraid of hard work. He rode well and fast and still found time to come up to the bench to be with her.

Rosa's Grandmother passed on and Rosa was left the little house. She eventually found work in a millinery, making hats. Life on the park bench had developed into a weekly meeting place with them both looking forward to Saturday evenings and Sunday afternoons. One could be forgiven for thinking life was idyllic, but as is often the case, these things seldom last for ever.

One Saturday, Rosa came running up the hill to see a stranger sitting on 'their' bench. As she drew closer she could see it was a man in uniform, an air force uniform, then he turned as she approached, he stood up laughing at her amazement - the man was Jack.

They sat for a long time just holding hands, it was then that Jack asked her to marry him on his return from duty. He was of course quite sure this damn war was not going to last for ever. He would write every day or as often as he was allowed. They kissed, they hugged, they laughed, and they cried, just how would she ever get by without seeing him.

Finally, they parted with the promise that she would visit their special place every day and would answer all his letters. When he came home they would be together all the time, never to be parted again.

For the first year there were many letters and two furloughs. On his second furlough he had given her a ring, a simple ring of lasting friendship, of love and a promise of good times to come.

But, for the next five years there had been nothing. Every weekend Rosa walked to the end of the road and climbed the little hill to their place, sat and prayed for him to come back. She had tried to get information from the air force but it seemed he had vanished from the face of the earth. There had been conflicting reports. His plane had been shot down over France, over Germany, over the Channel, but nothing forthcoming to help her. So, Rosa continued her sad walks to the bench and her talks to Jack, she knew he would hear her wherever he was.

The sun shone and Rosa climbed slowly up the incline, what a lovely day it was, and the park looked beautiful. Suddenly she knew what she would do, she started thinking about the little plaque on the back of the seat, she would have one made for her and Jack, just a little one with the date and their names. Perhaps a hundred years from now, a couple such as them would find each other and make this their special place.

The park bench came into view. Darn, there was someone there, a man sitting quietly, he had a dog with him, he was so still he could have been carved of stone. Rosa walked around to face him, his face had been horribly burnt and his eyes appeared to be sightless. Slowly the dog lifted its head and looked at her. Then quite suddenly Rosa started to cry, she looked again at the man. The blond hair was still the same, the way he leaned his head slightly to one side with that crooked smile - more pronounced because of the burns. He lifted his head and looked directly at Rosa. Rosa sat beside him, she knew he had been to hell and back, plenty of time for talk later.

With tears streaming down their faces and hands clasping each other Jack said :

"Rosa! Am I back home?"

"Yes, my Darling, we both are."

Foot Note

Love, Faith, Hope and Courage to go the distance, however far it takes you, are values worth striving for.

Judi Waller 2017

ANNIE'S MAN

He stood looking out on the vast expanse of nothing. It was dark and the fog was thick.

A cold night, yet somehow, he felt warm and at peace. He sensed rather than heard the footsteps close by.

"Evening Sir."

Well, if it wasn't old Tom Cavendish the local officer of the law.

"Evening Tom."

Tom had been walking the beat for all the years he could remember.

"Would you be alright sir?" Tom asked. "It be a cold night to be out."

"Thank you, Officer, I am fine."

He thought again of the events of the past twelve hours and of Annie lying in her own sweat. He had been so afraid and wanting desperately to run away. Was he a coward, was he? After all, like they said, too young - not man enough.

He looked into the void below and knew the muddy swirl of the Thames flowed below, a foghorn sounded in the distance reviving him from his thoughts. Yes, London was an eerie place in the dense fog at night, but he had lots to live for and he was man enough.

He knew the terrain well and had no difficulty in making his way back across the bridge to enter the hospital once again.

Now he felt good and no longer afraid. Full of anticipation and excitement, he quietly entered the room where Annie lay. She turned her head and smiled a soft smile full of happiness and in the crook of her arm, resting, was their infant son. He was a dad - nothing could hurt them now. He was man enough for anything. After all, he was Annie's Man.

J.W - 1993

MEETING A VIKING: A LOVE STORY

I first met my current husband at the end of 1979, early 1980. It is an interesting story in itself.

I had been married for twenty-seven years, had four lovely children and then found myself separated and lonely. It would seem that no matter the course, or who may have instigated the separation, it still remains a very sad and difficult time for both parties. Fortunately for me, my children were at an age that they either were working or married. With the exception of my youngest who was on the cusp.

We were living in Canberra ACT at the time and I was working as a manager of two real estate offices, so my hours of work were long and arduous. I was lucky, I had a very good friend, who sadly had recently lost her husband, and we fell into a pattern of meeting on a weekly basis, usually on a Friday evening. Sometimes we would go to a club, other times we would stay in and have supper and a few drinks.

During one of these sojourns at her house, Chris came up with the suggestion that we should take a cruise somewhere. At first I was not in favour. Not being, I thought, a cruising person, as I had spent a long trip on a migrant ship coming to Australia back in 1949. However, she was able to convince me that a migrant ship and a cruise liner of the day were of an entirely different ilk. With that suggestion in mind, I went home to think about the idea very strongly. I had not had a holiday in eight years, so this was going to be a sharp break from the continuous slog seven days a week, practically sixteen hours a day.

The following Friday evening Chris had all the brochures ready for me to peruse and for us to make choices. There was one trip that stood out - the ship left Sydney bound for Singapore with the first Port of Call Rabaul PNG, taking us through Japan and the inland sea, before flying back to Sydney - a good three to four weeks. The fact that the first Port of Call was Rabaul interested me. This was the place I had lived in my early married years and my first child had been born there, it was a beautiful place and my time there had been enjoyable. With the choice made to take that trip we proceeded to plan. My biggest problem was sorting out the time to take leave to coincide with the cruise ship's departure from Sydney. The length of time away was another difficulty and I might say somewhat of a shock to the boss man. However, with much cajoling and persuasive measures, he accepted the leave, and our bookings were made.

When the time came for us to go on leave, we departed from Sydney with various friends and relatives to see us off, what fun. On departure from Sydney the customs personnel took some time examining my passport. I heard one comment that it must be a new passport, which by the way was an English one not an Australian. Then I realised that I did not have an entry visa, as this was a new book, so the entry I had in perpetuity had not been transferred. On arrival in Brisbane, we took off for the United Kingdom passport office. I might say these people where extremely helpful and in a matter of approximately one hour I was duly endorsed. A deep sigh of relief and how fortuitous to have picked it up before our return. I guess we all must expect some hitches throughout life's journey.

As I said before, our first Port of Call was Rabaul, in New Britain PNG. What a lovely place to visit. I found it somewhat changed but still lovely - not so many war time wrecks visible in the harbour as when I lived there. Chris and I were not the sort to gather with the crowd on day excursions but rather to go our own way, thus getting to meet with the locals.

Having experienced the layout of the town we proceeded to go looking for China Town and the Marine Base where I had once lived. What a hot day it was. By the time we had searched, and failed, to find China Town we found ourselves walking down a road with what looked like empty buildings all shut up either side of us. Like so many tropical places, there is an afternoon siesta time and we seemed to be in the middle of it, everywhere was closed.

Just when we thought we could not walk any further we passed an open door with lovely cool air emanating from within. I called to Chris who was a little ahead of me.

"Hey, let's stop for a minute its cool in here."

When we stepped inside there was a fellow standing behind the front counter looking at what appeared to be a small motor in his hands, tall and shaggy, with a lovely smile. He immediately put the motor down on the counter and asked: "Are you off the liner that has just docked?"

"Yes," we replied. "And it is a very hot day, we have been walking for some time, looking for China town."

We learned his name was Mike and he invited us back into the office and served us cool water. Mike confirmed that it was indeed siesta time and every place would be closed for a couple of hours. He also confirmed that China Town had long gone, however, there were a few Chinese stores that would open after siesta. After some time, another young man came in, Ian Falconer, who worked for Mike. Mike suggested that Ian drive us around and show us the north shore where we could have a swim and a look around then take us back to the ship. What a lovely idea.

"Will you be coming too?" I said. Alas, Mike was too busy. To say I was a little disappointed would be an understatement.

The next few hours were a great deal of fun and we saw much of Rabaul and surrounds, and yes, a swim in the warm clear water of the sea. Ian took us to his home then to the markets, after which he took us back to the ship. Back on board we adjourned to one of the bars and just before visitors had to leave the ship Mike turned up. This pleased me very much as I was quite taken with this tall, rustic, quiet guy, whom I may never see again. We had time for a farewell drink then stood on deck to wave goodbye to two wonderful guys who had given us a lovely day and shown us a lovely place.

The next day we were cruising peacefully - idyllic could be the term. I said to Chris we should take some time out and go write a few cards to the folks back home, a good idea says Chris. So, with a collection of cards purchased in Rabaul at one of the Chinese stores, we took off to the writing room. On the spur of the moment, I decided to write a thank you note to Mike for making possible a lovely fun filled day.

"Sounds great," Chris said. "But how are you going to do that you don't have a surname or an address?"

Well, how hard was that? Knowing that his name was Mike and he was in an electrical business, I wrote a short note of thanks and addressed it to Mike, Rabaul Electrical Company, Rabaul New Britain. Stamped it and sent it off.

The rest of the trip was fun, we went ashore in Japan and China met some friends in the Foreign Affairs Department in Tokyo and eventually arrived in Singapore. After some few days in Singapore, where we stayed at the Hilton, we flew back home. Both agreed the highlight had been Rabaul and the relaxed fun day we had enjoyed so much. I wondered if Mike had received my thank you note.

Back to work, with many happy memories, both Chris and I talked so many times about that day in Rabaul and I thought often about a tall, rugged, quiet man with artistic hands, but life goes on.

Six Months later.

Our trip was fading into fond memories, and it was now Christmas time, with a round of parties and buying gifts which was always a tradition. Arriving home late at night, as was the norm for me, I found a heap of Christmas cards in my mail box. Amongst them a card from a company called New Britain Electrics, what a big surprise - it was from Mike (I had often wondered if he had ever received my note). Amazingly my note had gone to another company, namely Rabaul Electrics, but what I didn't know was that Mike's company was New Britain Electrics, hence the letter been pinned to the notice board in Rabaul Electrics. When Mike was visiting his mate, Ewan, he saw the note and suggested it may be for him, opening the letter solved the problem. I learned later that he was delighted to hear from me and promptly sent me a Christmas card, with words that still mean so much to me today.

So, six months on the board Mike finally received his mail. I have since learned that Mike is an avid reader of notice boards whenever he comes across one. He now had my address in Australia and the invitation to call whenever he came south.

Thus began a romance by phone. He rang most days on my private number at the office, which my staff knew never to answer should I be away from the office. Subsequently, Mike visited Australia for a couple of weeks and I was persuaded to visit Rabaul and join in a yacht race to Kavieng with him. We then made plans for me to take a year off from work and go up to be with him, work in his office and see how things worked out for us both.

Things went well for some time until the Volcanoes began to misbehave. The last eruption had been in 1927, so everyone thought we were very much overdue for another. The consequence of this was that business started to go bad and the whole economy of the place took a dive, at one stage I was the only white women in the town. It was at this time we decided to leave and that we would sail Mike's yacht (an old Boro built 42ft Ketch we named Bari-ke) home. Our trip back to Australia was not uneventful, but that's another story.

We left PNG in 1982. So much has happened since then. Mike and I married in 1991 and remain so today, still very much in love. Still enjoying each other's company, my dear friend Chris passed on having succumbed to a brain tumour while I was still in Rabaul.

To my dear friend, I thank you so much for talking me into that Cruise, all those years ago, and for the wonderful life we have had since.

(I dedicate the above recollection to an old friend –

Christine Stokes– till we meet again in a future life).

Not the end, but another time.

Judi Waller

28th August 2017

To my darling husband, Mike, for the words written in that Christmas card, and I quote: 'Next time I see you I will not let you out of my sight.' To this day I still have that card and cherish the words within.

LONG AWAITED TRIP TO LONGREACH

I once had a yen to take a trip into the outback of Australia, looking for some adventure. Finally, I did! After much deliberation I decided on a trip to Longreach, where the Qantas airline started from and where they have the Qantas Museum – a little taste of the Australian Outback.

There were four of us, but the trip didn't start too well. We had a major problem with the car. That was at 9:30am - not a good start. Even with the guys working on the motor, they still could not get it to run well. The local garage said they had no time to work on it and to go elsewhere, however it was thought to be electrical and the guys took off to the garage at the roundabout. Sometime later a phone call from one of the guys told us the problem was fixed and they were on their way back. My friend and I finished packing the van and we were ready to leave as soon as the men arrived back, with time enough to hitch the van to the car and off. Our time of departure was 11:30am - just two hours behind schedule. The problem, I believe, was a loose contact on one spark plug.

Three hundred and sixty-five kilometres to our first fill up at Dalby.

The ride to Dalby was uneventful and the guys took turns with the driving – we bought pies at Wamuran, then over the Black Butt range with a change of drivers after that. We got through to Dalby and met up with friends on their property, enjoyed a good night, a few drinks, a lovely meal and a lot of talk.

We spent a quiet evening enjoying the peace and quiet, solace after the trauma of the starting problems.

7th Oct, 2009, on awakening we prepared eggs and bacon on the fire, a good breakfast. Departure was timed at 8:05am.

Kogan was the first stop, where we asked the way to the Kogan Creek Power Station, fifteen K's down the road (Kogan Power Station and observation area). The Power Station is a 750 megawatt coal fired power station owned by CS Energy on the Darling Downs, (which according to research is enough to power almost one million homes and we were told it is the most efficient and largest coal-fired generating unit in Australia). Wow!! Interesting stuff. After spending some time looking into the history and the ilk we were on our way again, this time heading for Tara. However, not much to see in Tara. It's a very small and disappointing town with approximately two thousand residents. Its location is ninety kilometres north west of Dalby, Western Downs Region. We have heard since then that it has some lovely gardens and a vintage car museum. Well, we missed that.

We decided to head for Glenmorgan. This was a very nice town with some very interesting historic features, one of which is the Antique Car Museum along with an antique store - great to browse through. We had lunch by the old Railway Station and the Gaol.

The next stop was at Sarat – a really nice small town, home of the Cob and Co Museum and very well worth seeing. There's a large aquarium on entry with a rural vista drawn around.

At this point it would be interesting to note that all the roads we had travelled were very good with only some dirt going to Dalby and the Kogan Power station area.

We travelled the Warrego Highway to Roma, stopping just twelve kilometres past Roma to the west at a camping site in the grounds of an old Homestead. 'Meadow Bank' cattle property, Buneworgorai Creek (it means Muddy Water) and it had been operating for twenty-eight years. The result - a good night under the stars. The next morning, we were due to go through the homestead and we all agreed on an early morning rise.

Thursday morning, we rose early, breakfast and wash up, we were all ready by eight o'clock and waiting to go through the homestead. It was truly a grand experience. The tour cost $10 per head, but really worth it. The consequence was after the tour we were late leaving, but why bother with a tight schedule when viewing such worthwhile exhibits and history is something we were all interested in?

We arrived in Mitchell at 1.10pm – "Guess we won't make Longreach tonight." The country is really quite boring and not good for the driver – flat grain country and very hot – thank goodness for the cool nights and mornings. The clothes were getting somewhat grubby, and I suspected the bodies could do with a long hot shower.

Arrived Tambo, what a really lovely place, a different terrain with more mulga scrub. Saw some emu's, bustard (plain Turkey), a brolga and lots of horses - yes truly a lovely country. Stayed on the side of the Barcoo, a very pretty waterway. Come morning we breakfast and spent more time looking around. We saw the Qantas Crash site, took photos and saw lots of kangaroos. Still very flat country and hot driving. We changed drivers for a while so I get to sit in the front seat, it changes the perspective of how one looks at the terrain. We were making good time, despite the delays in looking around sight-seeing so to speak, but that was what it was all about. We arrived in Blackall mid-morning and tried to call on a friend, but to no avail, they must've been working or off visiting.

Our next adventure was to visit Scour Place or, to put it correctly, the Blackall Wool Scour, which is a collection of sheds containing shearing equipment. A history of sheep shearing and wool washing. The last remaining steam operated wool washing plant in Australia and a real live museum with links to Australia's past. Having spent some time digesting the history of the Blackall Scour, we picked up some fresh bread and had a lazy lunch. Once again, we were on the road, which was flat straight and very boring, but we did see some life - lots of emus.

Arrived at Isisford mid-afternoon. This was also a nice little place but still no mobile access – we needed a NextG sim card to work the mobiles. However, no problem we got to the Museum, where we were lucky enough to obtain a family pass, saving us money again. The Theatre show was excellent, the museum ordinary. Having spent some time enjoying the town and what it offered we head off expecting to make Longreach by that night, but we ended up bedding down three K's out of Longreach.

Saturday – A full day. First, up and into town to book the boat ride - picked up some bread – sent the boys back to van to put the fish in freezer, as we planned to eat dinner on the boat that night.

As soon as the boys got back we headed off to the Hall Of Fame - I had expected an all-day affair but was very disappointed. I had seen it many years earlier, but it had changed and not for the good. However, the Qantas Exhibition was excellent and I could have spent more time there. We had spent three hours in the Hall of Fame the rest of the time in Qantas, it could have been a whole day, but one never knows, there can always be a next time if needs be.

Back to camp and we were picked up for the Billabong Paddle Steamer ride – it was a full house. Forty minutes up the river then a return to a large open camp fire - what a brilliant night. Dinner was stew and bread, Apple Strudel with cream then Damper and Treacle with coffee and tea. The entertainment was a singer of Country Music Songs and Milton the Bush Poet who were both easy to listen to. Met two others from our camp site, Lila and Ian. Ian was from New Zealand and a bit staid. Lila, an older women, was great fun and full of life. However, it was the best night and greatly enjoyed by all.

Sunday morning and we were ready to leave Longreach at 8:30am to head for Combe, a very small town, but it was too early, and nothing was open. We took a little drive around then headed out to Emerald.

Emerald is a prosperous town located on the Nogoa River in the Central Highlands Region and a gateway to the sapphire gem fields. What a shame, no time to go fossicking, but maybe another time - this is a place worth spending time in. We saw the Van Gogh Sunflower Painting in Emerald's Morton Park. This is the world's largest reproduction of Van Gogh's painting and is a tribute to the town's history which used to be a sunflower producer. Other things to see if you have time are Lake Maraboon and the Emerald Botanic Gardens.

So, we headed for Carnarvon, go through Springsure and Rolleston. Lunch on the Carnarvon Road, about twenty K to turn off – we had Nachos for lunch with white wine. At the turn off the bitumen ends - what an awful road all the way to The Gorge, however it was all shut off and only opens six months of the year. We had to go back to the resort and decided to stay overnight - $72 for a four people van, what a rip off! We were set up by 3:45pm for a night in Takarakka Resort - it's rather misleading as it's only a bush camp. We lost power through the night, and it didn't come on again till the morning at about 10am.

Tuesday morning – we rose early had breakfast and set off to The Gorge, we walked through the moss garden then up to the art gallery, a distance of fifteen K's. On return there was a ranger up a tree trying to get a dead branch chopped down. We say: "A Koala up a tree with a chain saw!" Wow, two of us got through and they closed the track so the other two got trapped with the closure before and after. We finally got back to camp, with just enough time for a shower, then on the road again to Roma.

The trek out was hot, smoky, boring and a very hard drive - one hundred and ten kilometres to Injune then ninety to Roma – I would say the worst part of the whole drive. A truck passed and threw a stone which left a nasty mark in the windscreen. No

O'Brien in Injune, but then not much of anything, so on to Roma where once again we had mobile access. We picked up some fresh veg and fruit, found out where the O'Brien Glass was situated, go there to get a patch on the windscreen and then up the road to Meadow Bank working farm, just twelve K's out. It's very windy and there's heaps of fly's, we'd better keep the mouth closed. We settled down at the farm and met two people, Phil and Jan from Moree, and enjoyed Happy Hour with them. We had a late dinner of Prawns and Thai curry with rice, what an excellent meal. Well, its bed down and rest up for the morrow.

Wednesday – we were up early, had breakfast and spent two and a half hours going through the Museum with Don Tite - it is amazing, he had just about everything in there. However, the best is the Corn Stripper, what a machine. I had to go back and get a closer photo. Later we went into town to get the windscreen fixed and had a counter and a Guinness lunch in an Irish Pub. Then off to see the Big Rig. The Big Rig and visitors' information centre provides a professional service to visitors. There is an evening show which gives an insight to the history however, we could not stay for that, maybe next time.

Head back to the farm for an evening with everyone at our camp, we had a few drinks and met a new couple. I think the girl's name was Tracy but cannot remember the fellow's name, the couple Phil and Jan joined us as did the owners Don and Pat Tite. So, a pretty chatty night and lots of fun. We swapped email addresses, however we're very unlikely to hear from any of them - that's the way of it, it's quite a shame actually.

Thursday, left at 8:50am. It's a very cold morning but had a good farewell from new found friends. It's a very nice place to stay and I can highly recommend the stop over.

Next stop, Miles Historical Village and we had lunch on the side of the road - a nice grassy park beside the Historical Village.

Friday – 7:40am, we went through Jandowae. A quiet service centre near the Queensland end of the Dingo fence, it's a small rural town and a friend of ours was billeted there during the war. The country was improving and the weather was fine, not as hot as it had been. We head for Kingaroy Pass - a scenic lookout driving four kilometres on rough track, but worth the detour and plenty of room to turn. Boiling Springs lookout – Dingo fence. The drive through to Kingaroy was very lovely country and quite different from what we had been through. We fill up at Kingaroy – we have done 2,933K's.

Next stop Wondai. Between the towns of Murgon and Kingaroy, Wondai features mainly cattle and grain growing country and grassland between eucalypt forests.

Home – our round trip was over three thousand kilometres.

Hey! Going travelling? Take a trip to Longreach it's very informative lots of history and can be great fun. GO ON DO IT – YOU WILL LOVE IT. We did. We saw some sights, but many we didn't get to see. Maybe you will see more!

THE SAILOR

The Sailor on the deck at night, a lonely watch he keeps,

While snugly in their bunks below,

The crew and captain sleeps,

Then in the silence of the night he'll cry:

"it's 8 o'clock, and all's well ,"

Then to make sure that they awaken, he'll loudly ring the bell.

                                                Burt Russell 20/9/00

THE JUNKET OF THE SAILING VESSEL
S.V. ARIEL

FROM CAIRNS TO THE TORRES STRAITS

Skipper: Mike Waller

LOG: Written by Judi Waller (A Woman's Perspective)

The following is an insight to travels on board the yacht, Ariel Eight, as it was so named at that time. I have taken the words directly from our log as we proceeded to the Islands in the Torres Straits.

S/V ARIEL 1994

Having given you an insight to travels on land, maybe you would like to read about one on water.

We had at one time owned a yacht, several actually, though not all at the same time - just one at a time.

After sailing from PNG to Cairns and selling our 42ft steel ketch (Bari Ke), we purchased a small 33ft lidgard, a New Zealand built aluminium Sloop. This was a fun boat and, being smaller than the ketch, easier to handle in more confined coastal areas

Well, the story I want to tell is taken out of our hand written log, written by yours truly (then finalised by Mike) during a trip from Cairns to the Torres Straits. We had accepted a job doing installations throughout the Torres islands. There were two other people with us, but each had their own boat - both power boats and there will be mention of them throughout this narrative.

Prior to departure, we spent two solid weeks getting the yacht prepared, needless to say we were pretty dead beat before starting. We found some little things that needed fixing beforehand, not in the least our depth sounder, which was not working, so we had to wait for the shops to open to enable us to purchase a new one. This was good, we had it

jury rigged but it kept slipping back to show depth straight back however, it still shows us the fish, some I believe even show the type of fish – nothing like modern day technology

October: Sat 15th Depart Cairns Cruising Yacht SQUADRON at 1030 hrs. Picked up with Fletcher Christian and Katcher 111 at the leads. Turned off at No.4. Problems hoisting the main. Sea's choppy approx. 1.5mts. – sailing approx. 5Knts heading for Double Island – new G.P.S not operating. Winds approx.15 to 20 knots. Expected 25 to 30 knots S/East

Arrived Low Island 1830 hrs at last light. Anchored 4 mts water and turned in.

Oct. Sun.16th 0600 hrs start – head north from Low Isle turn to set the main – still having problems – then the motor warning sounds, no water getting through, Cairns harbour so dirty filter choked, remove choke all okay for now. Lose sight of Fletcher Christian and Katcher. The sails are set and heading for Cook Town.

Arrived Hope Island – Channel 1330 hrs picked up Katcher and heading for Cook Town. ETA Cook Town at 1815 hrs.

Everyone very tired both Phil (Fletcher Christian) and I pretty sick. Decide to make Monday a lay day enabling us to undertake some minor repairs and recoup. We eat aboard Fletcher – Mashed spuds cabbage carrot and corned beef apparently cooked in transit.

Oct.17th Monday - spend most of the morning cleaning the yacht discover bilge full of water so go on a hunt to find the problem.

Decide tanks leaking and seal the I/O's 1530 hrs. go ashore to ring up and post overseas Xmas cards.

Fletcher Christian having freezer problems and motor. Katcher more problems also. 1700 hrs back aboard Ariel V111 and we find the bilges full again, this time it's the gland on the motor dripping constantly, we will have to do repairs. Mike says okay now that we know we can fix tomorrow. Thus, we retire 2030 hrs to get a good night's sleep and an early start.

Tuesday Oct.18th – Awake 0630 hrs and make ready to sail – I am nervous about this leak, but Mike says we will fix it tonight at the Turtle Group. We pump out the bilges make coffee and generally get ready. Fletcher Christian and Katcher come alongside we decide to meet in Owen Channel. Then Fletcher loses power. I guess we aren't going yet. 0700 hrs Katcher comes over for Mike, must be electrical.

Now we wait and see what will happen, I would like to see another day to get the leak fixed.

0725 hrs finally and at last depart Cook Town, Mike has fixed Fletcher Christian Yippee.

We motor out and set sail, seas much better today and we are sailing nicely.

1010 hrs off South Bedford Cape very pretty country. Katcher calls to see how we are going then "Fletcher" calls he is 2 miles south of Flattery they are going on – we decide the Turtle Group too far, need the daylight to fix the leak.

Radio has been quiet for the rest of the day. Arrive Cape Flattery and drop anchor 1545 hrs – 3 yachts anchored we talk with "Troopship" they have come down from the Kimberley's looking for better winds – left for Port Douglas they should get a reasonable run through and it's a full moon or close to, one other yacht leaves also

The Bilges not too full, she's pretty dry this time, we did pump twice today. We had trouble with the motor again not getting water through – also trouble with the depth sounder, Mike's jury rig not working to well. I think our readings are straight back and sideways

(Wow, forgot to mention the porpoises we encountered just out of Cook Town, some very large, they stayed with us for some time under and over and all around what a display).

We make coffee and we start playing with the motor.

Wednesday Oct.19th awake at 0500 hrs in fact neither of us slept that well we rocked and rolled all night and the auto helm groaned and grunted along with the rigging.

Departed Cape Flattery 0600 hrs – needless to say did not get the leak fixed so still baling.

Made sail and head out towards Lizard to get a good run back to Howick - a very pleasant sail. Finally got the sails worked out for a downhill run.

Anchored Beswick lea side at 1615 hrs (we are running goose winged with a jokey pole on the headsail). Looks like another rocky night but it is pretty sheltered. Spoke with another yacht (Varguss) anchored Noble Island very interesting. Probably doing 8 knots this pm so look for a good run tomorrow should put us in the Flinders group.

Thursday Oct. 20th – 0600 hrs awake after a rugged night (Capt. Jack Von Rider you have a lot to answer for).

0655 hrs weigh anchor and head for Cape Melville – winds southeast 15 to 20 knots not as pleasant as yesterday. Meet up with 3 large yachts 2 going south 1 going north 3 0 of us in line at Barrow Point (1 called Team Trinida). We lose the wind, Main just sheared off and sunk.

 Round Cape Melville 1030 hrs Drop the Head Sail continue

with main only.

Approach Flinders Group, enter Owen Passage. Drop anchor 1430 hrs and what do you know still having motor problems.

Starting to take notice of coast line it really is magnificent and quite awesome. Yacht Storm Girl sloop anchored in lagoon looks pretty low water we stay out as we want an early start am. Wind is howling again.

Torres Express comes through the channel; this would be the one carrying our equipment. No sign of Katcher or Fletcher Christian, but they would have stopped here last night.

Hooray we have music. Mike fixes our new radio cassette at 1805 no radio – but at least music.

Friday Oct 21st 0545 hrs. Awoke at 0445 hrs, getting ready to weigh anchor. Departed Flinders Group Owen Channel 0625 hrs passed the trawlers fishing from the Torres Express at 0650 hrs. Out in the Bay heading 290 degrees, see a big shark alongside.

0700 hrs passed first light 0900 one barge going south, large tanker going north Yang Wing line cuts the corner taking us off course. Steering 280 degrees; abeam of unnamed light 1200 hrs. Very pleasant sailing now that the seas have dropped, still winds SE 10 to 15 knots

Abeam of Berkut 1430 hrs back in the shipping channel – keep a sharp look out those big ships can come upon you fast.

Winds have turned to Northeast very sad we will have to work harder, may slow us down. We can't make Morris Island we will try for Hay Island – looks good.

1615 hrs dropped anchor inside Hay Island in 17mtrs water 50mtrs offshore seas very flat – see Torres Express go through the channel will probably take us another 3 days maybe Monday now.

Sat Oct 22nd Started motor 0615 hrs. Solid anchorage but a bit bumpy pretty well protected - however still did not get much sleep.

0630 hrs Anchor up. 0635 hrs depart. Wow see a large banded sea snake off the port side looks ugly. Trouble with motor again Mike has taken thermostat out again, cut motor at 0830 hrs sailing again.

0900 hrs off Fife Island a trawler tucked inside. 1030 hrs abeam of Ellis reef marker.

1125 hrs Bow reef

1220 hrs Spoke with Hush Hush down from IT sailing south has the winds we had yesterday – recommend we look at Forbs Island we just may do that on the way back.

1330 hrs water witch light we are now motor sailing. 1750 hrs Cross sand bar into Lloyd Bay.

1900 hrs Drop anchor bottom of bay 5.5mtrs water, both dead beat.

Sunday Oct.23rd a bitch of a night Mike up several times - don't think he got much sleep at all. We will head for Portland Rhodes and maybe stop there to recoup still two days traveling for us.

0800 hrs up anchor heading north to get out of this shit of a bay. We pass Cho Yang Line at 1030 hrs heading south. We are approaching Weymouth Point.

1110 hrs Pass Resolution Rock just in front of Resolution Island. This is where Captain Bligh came ashore after being set adrift by Fletcher Christian. Going ashore for water then continuing his epic row North to Timor across the Torres Straits.

1200 hrs Dropped anchor in Portland Roads (short for Roadstead) all calm anchorages are called that.

We will now try to clean up. Mike had changed the impala in the motor while we were still out there. Hopefully the motor will now get us thru. Changed the main halyard. Halyard was stopped. Hoisted Mike to top of mast to cut down radar detector as rope stripped and hanging by a thread. Changed the topping lift.

Monday Oct. 24th – 0600 hrs up anchor – passed M.V. Exocedus, a prawn trawler, no one on deck must have dropped anchor and went below all nav: lights still on, no radio response.

0630 hrs leave Portland Roads

0635 hrs set the sails – a lot of water in the bilge hope that leak is not getting worse

0830 hrs off Eel Reef.

0940 hrs abeam of Forbes Island.

1010 hrs Abeam of Hazel Light – 2 ships in the channel one north bound Civic Lean or some such and one south bound M.V. Ionian Sea. Pass at 1025 hrs.

1045 hrs between Piper and Inset reef lights 1150 hrs off Marker Young reef next Inset

1225 hrs Moody Reef

1250 hrs Abeam Haggerstone Island making good time and a broad reach

sail.

1320 hrs Abeam of Clark Island light in the home island group.

1500 hrs Drop anchor in Margaret Bay a very nice little anchorage but not for long, have to manoeuvring as we drag.

Tuesday 25th Oct. 0600 hrs getting ready to up anchor, left Margaret Bay. Trawlers are coming back after their night's work. Looks like one yacht battling south too.

Heading for Bushy Island 45 miles away if winds prevail, should take about 9 hours eta 4pm.

0850 hrs Abeam of two Islands back in the shipping channel - about to change course slightly. Seas bad 2 metres short and choppy – Don't like this (approx. 2 to 2 and half metres) - (too rough to write).

Dropped anchor 1500 hrs off Bushy Island. 7 metres of water not good but at least will give Mike some respite. I am quite useless in big seas with 20 to 25 knot winds Gusting to 60 knots is pretty frightening.

Bushy Island is just a sand cay out in the middle of know where. – What a night and such a long one it seemed. We hung back with the winds howling our anchor chain and rope almost perpendicular, how we hung on I think was a miracle or some divine providence but we did and we got through the night, we did lose the wind gage off the mast. I would venture to say the worst night thus far.

Wednesday 26th Oct. Winds and seas still up pretty frightening. Mike reefs in the main we depart 0700 hrs.

1200 hrs we pass Cape

1430 hrs Buzzed by plane, Coast Guard from Thursday Island, it seems we have been reported missing, overdue, it was like a Guardian Angel out of the blue and such a nice friendly voice (Small Green yacht below please identify). (My reply -this is Alpha Romeo India Echo Lima - Ariel eight, I even surprised myself at being able to recite the phonetic alphabet without hesitation, very proud.) We tell him we have had problems but we can make TI okay. Motor smells bad worried about a possible gas leak from refrigeration. We hear TI Coast guard call Fletcher Christian and report our sighting (Police get it wrong and call Fletcher Christian) – We call Fletcher Christian nice to hear Phil's voice.

Katcher 3 calls up we give him our ETA 1900 hrs they said they would stand by channel 16 in case they are needed.

They sight us in the channel and come out to guide us in – Drop anchor 1835 hrs - what a relief from such rough weather.

The guys had been there since Sunday lunch time – by Tuesday were getting pretty worried hence the report that actioned the search. Thank God it was short lived. I ring my Mum on Phil's sea phone. All ok at home.

Thursday Oct. 27th, We wake late 0700 hrs, we sure needed the rest such a peaceful night. So now the big clean up and Mike back with the motor seems the smell may have been one battery over cooking.

Apparently, the guys had some problems also – Phil had a fire in his motor from the insulation foam, seems not fireproof after all.

Well we are all here safely now to organise to get some work started.

Most of the day spent getting ship shape again – wrote some letters went ashore to Thursday Island and made some phone calls.

It would appear that we have real trouble with the motor and battery, seems the alternator is stuffed more cost – currently relying on solar power to charge the batteries.

Dinner aboard Ariel 8, Phil and Dave joined us two types of chicken curries – plenty of port, consequently we retire late.

Friday Oct. 28th Wind appear to have dropped, some of the gear has arrived and barged across to Badu Island. However, still some equipment to arrive as this is not sufficient to complete the job. We go ashore to get a new battery and hopefully fix the alternator.

Winds have come up hope they settle down we don't want a rough crossing.

Saturday Oct. 29th – 9 weeks to Christmas. Very quiet today the winds have dropped seas like glass, hopefully the equipment will arrive today then we can leave for Badu Island while the seas are down. Yes and start Work!

Sunday Oct 30th – prepared to depart to Badu Island up at dawn start motor 0540 hrs 0555 hrs proceed down Chanel - position 10.35.47 142 14.24. There seems to be some confusion as to which route to take finally made up our minds.

0720 hrs pass Good Isle with gun turret on point, heading for West Island water like a mill pond. We see a few large turtles poking their heads up to take a look they keep their distance.

Cross Prince of Wales channel behind large tanker.

West Island about 112 miles away 2 to 2 and a half hours for us doing approx. 5knots the main is up but it is pretty useless.

1055 hrs West Island such a lovely bay but unfortunately unable to stop this time the boys have been here a couple of hours having a great time swimming diving and waiting for us.

Proceed to the Barry Island group start of channel and up to Badu Island. The boys are waiting in a very nice little bay drop anchor 1410 hrs. Having decided to stay the night we have a BBQ and go for a swim.

Monday 31st Oct. 0600 hrs – We awake after a restless night not such a good anchorage. Phil is aground and we are close, the coral reef looks far too closely, it will be a while before we can get down the channel.

0800 hrs – Underway and heading for Badu Island going pretty slow worried about rocks and shallow water. Let the barge go thru we are in 5mtrs of water.

Fletcher Christian already at anchor 0930 drop anchor in 3.1 metre of water hope it's enough to accommodate the tide especially after last night's and this morning's efforts. See Phil and Dave head ashore – this is where the work starts. Took a run ashore, must get a motor for the dingy so that we can be a bit more independent.

The most prominent feature of Badu is the very large very ornate cemetery on the foreshore, quite well kept and almost all stark white. We took a walk through and it was amazing to see how many babies - either at birth or during their first year. We went to another Island off the side of Moa where we were supposed to meet with someone, unfortunately he had already left. So we return to Badu. We were in Dave's boat, so it only took 15 minutes to get there.

The Materials have not yet arrived the barge that was in this afternoon was not carrying anything for us. But Phil is the organiser – we just sit and wait a good time to fish. Caught one small parrot fish guess it will do for bait.

Tuesday 1st November 1994. 0530 hrs awake everything

so still 0630 hrs get up- it's going to be a very hot day after such a quiet night in which we hardly moved, we are well rested. Mike changed the anchor anyway just to be on the safe side. Seas come up with the wind and we toss around. We end up going ashore no outboard so we row, hard yakka. On land we get a lift into what constitutes The Town!

With Mick from Cook Town Works Qld. Roads - they are doing the airstrip I guess they are going to open it again. No Post office – Council Chambers Pub and Trades Store. We go to Council Chambers, Phil and Dave are there nutting out what has to be done, but they want something done first Phil says: "A little greedy this crowd." Back aboard we await the barge.

Phil and Dave go around the sights the guy from TI turned up again all of this is so frustrating and such a waste of money. (Still No Barge).

Hear the TI Police talk with Helicopter - it would appear that there are some people stranded with a broken motor near Harvey Rocks. Katelyn responded she is a government fishing boat half hour away. Customs helicopter was running out of fuel only 5 to 10 minutes left to make a dash for land, apparently all seemed to end up okay.

WHO WON THE MELBOURNE CUP?

"It went to England."

Still no Barge – we hear them talking though - and Mike seems to think he knows the new skipper on the Shelbourne Bay.

Wednesday 2nd November 0600 hrs arise – STILL NO BARG

Well the Barge comes in – Ted the skipper is indeed known to Mike a real mate we go aboard and have coffee while it unloads. YIPEE, now we may get some work done.

Back aboard Ariel at lunch time – Mike leaves and much to my disgust I have to stay aboard on my own while the guys do the rounds to drop off equipment needed at each job site.

Thursday 3rd November 1994

Most of the day from 0630 hrs was spent ashore – boy we really worked hard digging trenches in the heat is not much fun.

Friday 4th WORK

Saturday 5th WORK

Had a nice shower at Richards (the Council man's house on the hill) he is not using the house at the moment - lucky us.

Sunday 6th November – This was supposed to be a lay-day However Phil comes over to tell us we are going to St. Pauls today. No preparation we go ashore to assist Phil loading Fletcher Christian.

We up anchor – 1030 hrs.

1200 hrs Abeam of Kubin. Kubin is the name of the people on Moa. Try to round the point, Sth Point too fast a current running it is pushing us out, we go in and drop anchor behind the rocks just off the reef.

Dropped anchor at 1500 hrs. Have some lunch and wait the turn of the tide. Katcher calls but is unable to hear our response. Finally get round the point 1620 hrs but it is still heavy going, only averaging about 2 to 3 knots.

We cut the corner too close and tip the reef; Phil and Dave come out and guide us through the reefs.

A bad time of the day, we can't see the reefs we hit another on the topside near the break to entrance – no markers it is a visual thing. Finally get through and drop anchor 1810 hrs.

Both tired and more than a little sunburnt.

Phil comes over in the dingy he is returning to Badu 0500 hrs in the morning to pick up cement to finish bases here.

Monday 7th November 0600 hrs awake a pretty rocky night but none the less had a pretty good night's sleep. All the reefs are exposed its low tide looks awful, certainly not a big entrance.

Phil has left for Badu and Dave is over at the wharf looks like he is aground. I gather he will be over soon to take us ashore to start work.

We row ashore – have coffee with Dave then walk to council where we pick up a truck and some islanders, drop equipment at sites then leave them to dig the holes, by the time Phil gets back from Badu we are well under way. Phil and Dave leave for TI we continue working, not good, so very hot

Knock off around 1630 hrs. – Very low tide worried about grounding not a lot of water as it is.

Go ashore the boys do not turn up so start work, carry the conduit have not walked so much, so constantly. Check all the sites do some more to the first house says I can wash tomorrow.

Tuesday 8th November, 0630hrs, not a good night!

Phil and Dave away so we go ashore to get our side done, very hot, came back to the boat middle of the day. Put up the awning over the cabin area, makes things a mite cooler. Mike decides to change the hatch around to accommodate the weather – it does make a difference round the other way but how long it will stay unfinished is another story.

Phil and Dave get back – heaps of mail for us mainly from the bank but there was one Christmas card from Cousin Brenda in the UK. We go back ashore and set the 1st unit in the ground.

Wednesday 9th November.

Not a good night again, very rocky makes it hard for a day's work ahead and not much sleep. Now to make matters worse the stove has packed it in, nothing to boil water in for a hot cupper.

We get another two slabs done today, plus the electrics, so some progress has been made.

The Barge comes in tomorrow. We shall probably go back to Badu to complete those there. Very Hot, very tired and dirty. We got a little fresh water today – the water situation is not good. However I was able to do some washing at Frances's house. He is the eldest person in this place, 72 years old and lives with one daughter, a teenager who gets a carers pension to look after him, and he has one small adopted son, his niece's child, an unmarried mother, he has applied for adoption which will be finalised next year. I found him a very interesting person.

Thursday 10th Nov. Go ashore and finish last slab.

Up anchor at 1130 hrs, through the reef at 1150 hrs, pass the barge at 1210 hrs, the seas are pretty heavy going, none the less we have a good run. Round South Point at 1400 hrs, we experience a wind change to North Easterly: seas moderate giving us a much easier run down to Kubin. Sight the Barge astern quite a way behind, he will probably beat us into Badu. Abeam of Kubin at 1520 hrs.

We slowed down to negotiate shallow ground and dropped anchor 1610 hrs. The Shoalhaven Bay is in, Ted comes to say hello.

We beat the barge in, so Ted has to move to make way for the Torres Venture – Phil at the same time. Both Phil and Mike go ashore to unload the barge. Ted comes over to spend some time with us, we drink a full bottle of scotch WOW! It is nice to feel secure with very little movement. Had a good night's sleep – how much due to Scotch and how much the safe anchorage?

Friday 0600 hrs After a good night's sleep.

11th Nov. Spent most of the morning on the barge, caught some sardine fish for bait – watched a video then went to help in assembling the first toilet hut.

Took on several gallons of water almost full now complements of the Shelbourne Bay. Ariel sits better in the water now, more stable.

We get the first hut assembled and return to Ariel - go over to the barge cook tea for Ted had a lovely hot shower (what a treat) I cooked Coral Trout, Chips, Peas and pikelets to follow.

Watch my video of Natalie Cole and the start of the Last of the Mohicans, get too tired so go back to Ariel to return for the night. (There was a Disco at the Pub tonight, but no sound reaches us).

Sat 12th Nov. 0530 hrs awake - we had rain during the night. Go ashore at 0630 hrs to Richard's house and do the washing for us and Phil too. Then on to second council's house and assemble that one.

Dave comes over from St. Pauls with two of the boys pretty rough over there we are probably lucky that we left when we did.

Mike returns to the boat to get some more equipment takes Dave and the boys back to the bay, Fletcher Christian has dragged anchor so they shift the boat and make fast. Mike returns to Williams House. Phil and I have just about finished his hut. Rang Ailsa but Paul away still will try again tomorrow.

Back aboard Ariel - see the Shelbourne Bay has departed.

Finished work for the day at 1700 hrs. now we get sorted for tomorrow's work.

Pub not open, we heard the disco drank the place dry so the pub is really the Pub with No Beer.

Sunday18th, Another full day of work. The winds pretty strong still and the seas outside are still up.

Rang Ailsa again but Paul is still not back.

We really are getting on like a house on fire not much left to do. Have the experts coming in on Tuesday to screen the assembly - 3 different types so 3 different company's 2 from Brisbane and 1 from Melbourne.

Rang Ailsa again and hooray Paul answered the phone, it's okay for Credit at the chemist so hope Paddy can get it on the charter flight. Phil comes over for dinner showered at Richard's place and still no beer.

Monday 14th – Did some more washing as we were working at Richard's house, never miss the opportunity.

Most of the places are okay, except the Pig Pen up the hill, which is disgusting we all dislike working there.

All quite tried to-day so finish up around 1430 hrs. Back to the boat for a sleep and relax. The Guys from South will be up tomorrow to check the installations.

Tuesday 15th To-day we had three reps one for each type of unit for the finished article to be commissioned.

Gus from Melbourne for Roto Loo. Neil from Brisbane the Dumas and idiot from Brisbane, for the Red Worms. They take off for Kubin and Phil goes with them he will be gone for two or three days.

Wednesday 16th 0630 hrs Ashore at 0700 hrs fix the light at Richards's house and did the washing. Problem at the Church no bits to finish and some dispute as to which side the light goes. Back to Richards to ring Phil now we have to shift light the wrong side of door opening.

Back to boat for lunch. Still no sign of Dave he is supposed to come over to-day we find out he is at Horn Island. He is supposed to get the step treads.

Manage to speak with daughter, Jacquie, and spoke to Andrew Eggleston, accountant.

Thursday 17th Nov. It appears that Phil has blood poisoning and an ulcer near the bone on his leg – so cross if he had listened to me this would not have happened, I guess it will be a week or more before he gets back.

We complete Williams's electrics and the Church; Dave turns up but no step treads it seems they are still in Cairns. We are all dissatisfied with the whole set up, Mike and I are committed, however the first bit of money came through so there is hope for the next progress payment and we have to stick it out. Finish early again, we will get stuck into what we can tomorrow and hope for the best. Spoke with Tess our next-door neighbour all is fine back there.

Friday 18th Nov. Go ashore 0730 hrs, Dave spends a lot of time on phone to Phil and his telecom mates, it seems he will go onto Sabai and get the bases laid before the wet sets in. We have finished Richard, William and the Church. Jacks also as far as the electrics go. However Dave puts on a paddy, so nothing much else gets done. These men and their baby tantrums - must be a childhood thing. Get one hole cut and one unit in. Dave breaks the bit in a paddy, throws the pop riveter away, we decide we would be better off without him, we return early.

Saturday 19th Nov. Dave pulls alongside he is off to Horn Island to load the Barge. (That was a sheer waste of time his coming over at all). We go ashore and install Jacks Dumas it takes some time but we managed it.

We now have only two to complete as far as our interest goes, most work that we are doing now is to assist Phil. Try to ring Phil but engaged all the time eventually give up and head back to the boat.

Sunday 20th Nov. A real day of rest, we do not go ashore but relax all day. Do a few jobs on Ariel. We then decide to take our first two Chloroquine in readiness for Saibai. However I have trouble with the second tablet it gets stuck, my throat gets worse as the day goes by - can I have reacted to the tablets? Spend the rest of the day sleeping.

Monday 21st Had a very bad night my throat is really bad; we go ashore to get some work done call into the clinic – no sister there till later in the afternoon. Have a talk with Doctor on TI he says to leave off Chloroquine it's not necessary but does not think it's a reaction just a coincidence and that it is probably viral, so they can do nothing more than I am already doing.

By lunchtime I have had it, so we return to the boat after 1130 hrs; I sleep the rest of the day. Feel pretty bad.

Tuesday 22ndStill feeling pretty ill but decide to go ashore anyway – I didn't wish to stay aboard alone. We have finished the electrics so all we are doing is Phil's bits and pieces – as much as we can anyway.

We came back to the boat fairly early again, still feeling poorly.

Wednesday 23rd Nov. Back ashore and still feeling bad – get some of the doors done but we break the pop rivet gun , Phil's does not work either and neither does Dave's – this one was Mike's. So that puts pay to that. We also find out that Phil will not be back today; however they will both be back tomorrow. Decide to call at the clinic hoping to see the sister – still bad. Sister takes a swab to send off to TI very nice girl, Jenny. They also get Mike in and dress his tropical ulcers with a new moist method, Jenny has just come back from a seminar in Cairns. Mike is the first for her to try it on. Hope it works. We go back to the boat for a rest.

Weather is up again and it's pretty windy and blustery inside but still good. We hear a call for Ariel Eight on radio 16 - its Ted on Shelbourne Bay coming down the channel, so we gather up the washing also the shower gear and head for the barge. Thoroughly enjoyed another hot shower, at the same time do some washing and pick up some extra drinking water and would you believe watch a video - The Man Without a Face – Mel Gibson, really enjoyed it. Ted decides to stay the night so we are invited to cook tea and eat aboard. Vegies Steak, sausage and onion gravy, with ice-cream and fruit salad - a rare treat. They will be gone before we rise in the morning, it was good to see the old Ted again. But we have not repeated our Whiskey Bender thank goodness.

Thursday 24th Nov. Well Shelburne Bay has gone so are our Batteries out of sync with the Freezer Mike left it on so hand start and leave it run we will go ashore later today after we have charged the Batteries.

Take the rest of the washing ashore to Richard's place also the stove for Henry to put back the inner valve.

Expect Phil and Dave Back today – but the weather is up early they may not get to TI early enough to make the run to Badu.

TeLei Two left Badu two days ago and we hear today it sunk off Ascension Island - very sad.

Friday 25th Nov. Finished all electrics except Jayes, we have to do extra on circuit breakers our replacement Tractor is F………. ed not even Bonked just plain F……ed. Looking for Henry with stove and the coffee maker. Winds, 20kts - Seas 1.5mtrs, S.E.

This is Mike writing as I am feeling very poorly.

Saturday 26th Nov. 0700 hrs Start at the Church – Finish Merve – Finish. Pig Pen – Finish (The Pigpen nickname for the dirtiest place on the island). Williams – Finish. Jacks now on. Richards – Finish. Went out to the Thiess Camp – Water Drillers – in the bush - what a great set up and the boss supplies their beers, wow.

Three Gratis bores in town this may solve their water problems back to finish William's house. Met a nine year old full of knowledge knows everything about everybody. Well that's a nine year old for you. (This is Mike's writing I am having trouble, very sick). Then there comes a major problem a ten year old lad comes walking past the house we are working on with a fish spear nicely embedded in his upper arm muscle. Mike cuts the shaft off with the hacksaw but couldn't cut the barbs. Chopper comes in and takes him to TI Haus Sic – Waste of a good Fish Spear, his words, says Mike - I guess his way of getting past it. A brave little fellow.

Mike went to work to do the step treads but had to cancel. Judi now worse very sick.

Sunday 27th Judi not well at all have to cancel the work and get back to the boat. Judi running a high fever, dosing with disprin but not working.

Monday 28th Dave out to Saibai

Judi had a bad night still with fever. Packed a travel bag and organised a flight to Cairns for Judi, first trip to clinic had Mikes wounds dressed and checked Judi out. Mike rang a friend, Pat Pidgeon, and organised Judi to stay there while in Cairns under Doctors orders. Mike now left to organise the work side while Judi off to La La Land.

Below Mike's entry in the log – 1400 hrs load patient onto tractor our only local means of transport and off to place Balus.

1420 hrs arrived UZU Air 1445 hrs arrived UZU Air 1500 arrived Air North

1515 hrs arrived Cairns Charter 1530 hrs Arrived Air North Rang Fallon Air - would you mind waiting 15 mins

1545 hrs arrived UZU Air

1600hrs arrived Fallon Air finally found Badu Island

1610 hrs Judi flew out to Horn Island where hopefully the flight west was waiting to Cairns at 0715 hrs

2000 Hrs Tried Seaplane call but no connection. Readied yacht for tomorrow early, Dave in Saibai with U/S motor

From here on in Mike handles the yacht on his own and this goddam log. Well suppose that is nothing he hasn't done before.

Tuesday 29th 0500 hrs Fletcher Christian Calls to Mike: "Are you awake?" 0600 hrs Mike ups anchor 5knots NE with a very Low Low tide Heading out of Badu Island down the channel and up to Kubin. The self-steering was working well running into a 3kn current against a battle to be abeam of Kubin 0810 hrs tucked inside the reef –100mts to avoid headed current Coast Watch over the top at 500 ft.

Phil radioed 7Kn at Point, Reach South Point and headed out Wow! 7 knots backwards. 0950 hrs. 1010 hrs Anchored behind reef

1100 hrs up anchor set all sails head for Dollar Reef with motor. Tacked back at 1210 hrs past point 200mts. Abeam St Pauls. 5mile off reef turned in. Dropped sails anchored 1215 hrs 200mts off ramp mid channel

Set about to rebuild yacht. My one and only bottle of Chilli Sauce smashed on carpet. What a mess, pleased the BOSS is not here to see this one.

Put the ship back together winds N.E 10knts seas slight.

P.S Do worms get seasick.

Sea Phone call from Judi 1958 hrs. 6mins.

(Was nice to talk with Mike, how is he managing on his own?)

Wednesday 30th 0600 hrs Work, Work, and more Work – low, low, water in the lagoon no rain, wind 5 to 10 knots East (sea phone call Judi 1950 hrs 7 mins)

Thursday 1st Dec 1994 Another big low tide. Barge came in with 60,000 Litres of water as no water on the island.

1200 hrs Phil off to TI . Now finished St Pauls. Friday the 2nd December (RIP Father).

Cleaned ship, sorted gear. Had some lunch. Up anchor 1330 hrs. Out through reef. Tide dropping, Wind .5-10 East. Seas calm. Under motor – main course 120 degrees for Mt. Earnest Island. 1500 hrs Seas slight course 120 W.S 10E. 1530 hrs crossed V R shoal 5 Mts 1545 current s-n 6 knots North

1600 hrs anchored in 5 mtrs water 200 meters off beach, tide falling wind against tide big swell. (7min sea phone to Judi)

Saturday 3rd Dec. 0630 hrs miserable night very animated anchorage up anchor

0700 hrs motor to Gettula Island wind 10 knots E seas 8 metres anchored 1870 hrs. Slight swell rounding island . Tide rising, Wind against Tide again and rolling. 1600 hrs up anchor move north end of island between Suarji island into the straits more benevolent anchorage.

Sunday 4th December No phone last night

0600 hrs Sky to the north black its rain. 0810 Sea phone call 5mins Judi. 0900 hrs NE winds 10 knots. Two Crocks on sandbar watching. Waiting for Fletcher Christian read one whole book today Rang Judi 1900 hrs.

Monday 5th December Waiting 1400 hrs contact with Phil anchored 1500 hrs. From Horn Island GPS bag from TI Post Office.

Continuing with the 5th 0600 hrs have coffee 0700 hrs up anchor headed 0230 degrees Cape Islet 0710 hrs broke Top Halyard off Savars Is Port. Used topping spinnaker lift. Wind E 10K Main/Jib 7knots calm seas.

1130 hrs abeam Cap Is.5n mile radio Dave course change 330 degrees to Gabba Island

1200 hrs abeam wind N.E 10 k seas calm course 359 Main/Jib 8 knots magic sailing.

1530 hrs anchored west end Saibai Island in passage will attempt heads at low water tomorrow 6.3mts called Dave. (Great sail touched 11.1 knots)

Tuesday 6th December. 0630 hrs Still no low tide. Where are they when you want one Work – Work – Work!

Wednesday.7th December Let me tell you about Saibai Island – the western end of the town lives them f……ing Papuans, still in

Australian built Houses, God knows whether or not they are on the dole.

New Guinea is 1.5 miles across the strait like Bribie Passage, their all brothers and commute back and forth, but PNG side is across the track.

7th December continued - The sun sets are magnificent, and Duan Island lies west of us. Saibai is very flat and very low lying about 1 metre above high tide. Swamp at the back of the village. S.P. Beer is $60.00 per Carton Australia. Cheaper than Australian beer and slip across the channel to PNG.

Dave in my estimation would have to be the most inconsiderate and selfish Bastard I have ever come across (bar none).

Thursday 8th December Phil arrived - Work – Work – Work

Friday 9th December ditto – ditto - ditto -

Saturday 10th December Capt Phil has broken two ribs fell down the engine hatch of his boat. Doesn't want a sneeze or jokes.

Sunday 11th December Number 6 last one. No Rain Yippee

Monday 12th.December Final bits and wash up Lat 69 degrees 22 min 56 secs. Long 142 degrees 36 mins 58 secs

Tuesday 13th December 0100 hrs Judi and Paddles

Sign on Church at Lutheran Saibai:

"Where there is Death

there is Hope"

Me No Savvy

Now with me (Judi) back on board and the work finished we can end this missive and head for a joy ride or rather sail.

A LEAP OF FAITH
(Story - but a true happening)

The day was glorious mild and sunny. We were tied 'stern to' next to the boat ramp in Lae Harbour and alongside a Yacht named Calysta. Percy sat on the Seagull. For those that don't know the seagull is a small outboard motor which we had attached to the transom of our yacht Bari-Ke – and, as an aside, this little gem of an outboard was in fact invented by a woman. Well! I had to mention that didn't I? Percy was a Siamese Cat, a good companion at sea. Anyhow here I was in the galley, making preparations for a meal, while Percy sat on the Seagull eyeing the shore.

The yacht was gently moving back and forth with the movement of the tide, what a lazy feeling.

We had had such a rotten night before, when the weather came up, creating havoc all around. We had to radio some of the yacht owners to get themselves down to the marina and save their boats. We cast off the stern line and went out dragging two anchors where we stayed for the rest of the night, just circling the harbour and trying to keep out of the way of the larger ships coming and going.

Unfortunately, Percy had jumped aboard Calysta moored alongside us. The boats where jumping up and down so much it was too difficult to reach in and grab him, so we had to leave without him. I put out a call for anyone seeing Percy to save him for me. However, that did not happen, as on returning the next morning we could hear him calling right across the harbour, and as soon as we tied up he jumped aboard. I gather very pleased to be back or pleased for us to be back.

Unfortunately, the rotten night had taken its toll on our friends' little yacht which had been tied a little further up beside the slipway. Consequently, being so close to the cement ramp, the yacht had been pushed onto the ramp and holed. Once again emergency repairs get the yacht out of the water and repair the damage.

So here I was preparing food and Percy eyeing off the shore, the next thing there was this rather large splash, Goodness! What was that? I thought a big fish had jumped. I came up on deck fast to see what had made the splash. Percy was gone from his perch and all I could see was a bow wave circling the yacht. On circling back to the stern, I could see it was Percy. He had swum right round the boat and was heading for the wall. Who said cats couldn't swim?

I called to Karen who was working on the repairs of her damaged yacht.

"Hey Karen, Percy's in the water!"

"Well go and get him then," she replied.

"How can I, you have the Dingy,"

"Oh, Okay!"

So, Karen had to drop what she was doing and get the dingy pulled around to where Percy was. At this point Percy had reached the wall and was anchored with all four paws, claws extended, clutching onto the wall and screaming like a young child.

(Picture, if you will, a cartoon of a cat just been electrocuted with all its fur spiked out, mouth wide open and the cartoonist emulating a scream – well that was the look of Percy). Karen reached him and pealed him off the wall, how he never clawed her to bits is amazing, (Karen was wearing the briefest of bikinis).

The result was an hour spent cleaning up poor Percy, to get the muddy water off him, and back to his old self.

Certainly, a leap of faith!

THE HUNGRY SEA

While on the subject of cats, the following is a little story related to me by a friend, Sue Bett. Sue has given me permission to include it in this book, I believe it happened to a friend of hers.

Huge waves tossed the little sailing boat as the man struggled to keep her on course. Lightening ripped through a sky as dark as a plum pudding.

A marmalade cat sat in the cockpit trying to maintain balance and dignity. She glared at the man as if the rolling motion was his fault. The cat could not escape below - the hatch was sealed against the onslaught of salt water constantly washing over the boat.

"I hate cats," shouted the man above the roaring wind. "And you most of all."

The cat was a constant reminder of a broken relationship. His partner of some four years had left him and taken everything except the one thing he needed least – the marmalade cat.

The little boat lurched, battered by the big seas. The water tore at his body. He lost balance and desperately fought to regain his grip on the tiller. His safety harness bit and bruised his body as he looked about to assess the damage.

The cat was gone.

For a moment he felt relief. The last living memory of his partner swept unceremoniously overboard. Why then did he suddenly feel a pang of sadness, remorse? What the hell? He was fighting to stay alive and here he was feeling sorry for a cat! He had never even stroked it.

Another huge wave exploded on the deck. He was shoulder deep in foaming turbulence. Struggling to wipe the salt water from his face he could not believe his eyes.

The cat was back. Dumped from the crest of the wave, almost at his feet. The man watched, mesmerised, as the surge swept the scrabbling, indignant and sodden bundle back to the edge.

He snatched it from the deck and shoved it inside his wet weather jacket. He could feel it shivering and mewing.

The storm abated as quickly as it had arrived. The man took the cat below and rubbed it vigorously with a towel. As he heated some milk, he realised he was smiling.

Exhausted, he connected the auto pilot and fell on his bunk. In the eerie calm that follows a storm he could hear the cat lapping up the milk. He drifted off to sleep, but awoke later to a sound like a well-tuned and gentle motor. A purring, vibrating, orange bundle was contentedly curled up on his chest.

THE ANTIGONISH

When I came home last night at three,

The man was waiting there for me,

But when I looked around the hall,

I couldn't see him there at all!

Go away, go away, don't you come back anymore!

Go away, go away, and please don't slam the door…

by William Hughes Mearns 1922

WALKS ON HIS TOES!

It was evening. The lake glistened in the fading sun light as she walked towards the only empty park bench, a few moments alone will help to settle the sadness. The air was cool and she shivered, pulling her jacket closer to her.

Why had she come here? The hospital on the lake was no longer there, all gone, they had pulled it down some years before.

Memories, they weigh heavy. How long had it been? Only weeks, still it seemed like yesterday and the hurt in her chest had not eased.

The year was 1984, the news was good, her daughter had delivered of a baby boy – her first Grandson. The birth had been by caesarean so there had been some anxiety, however all was okay and they travelled south to join the family for a christening, such a happy occasion. There were the usual hugs, laughter and this little bundle of joy being passed around as the centre of attention.

She sighed and looked across the lake, the tears in her eyes putting a different wavy look to the darkening waters as the winter sun dropped further behind the surrounding mountain range.

Other than that first encounter with her Grandson she struggled for the memories. She missed so much. Their travels from one end of the country to the other had kept them some distance from seeing all the family during those early years. Would she have done anything different had she known the future? Probably not.

They named him Craig – it was to be Jonathon right up till the time of his birth. Why the change, who knows? But he suited Craig and he really made a better Craig than a Jonathon. Now why did she think that, was it something someone had said? Maybe.

Once again, she closed her eyes and saw him taking his first steps, such an amusing sight. He had a big head, so he looked top heavy and walked on his toes. He had a big grin on his face. Looking at the world from a different perspective had given him much pleasure. We were all sitting on the floor watching and laughing and he was so enjoying the attention as children often do.

From that day onwards he appeared to walk on his toes. Many times she placed her hands on his shoulders. Get off the toes, she would say and he would look at her and smile. He grew to have size eleven shoes, a very handsome young man and very tall, towering above her. He must have been a throwback somewhere as both his parents were short in stature.

Memories can be cruel, and they can be happy. His early school years were a big part of his life she had missed, having moved to Cairns. It was to be nine years before they returned to Brisbane and during that time she had seen her Grandson only a handful of times, such a large gap in a child's life.

Craig was an intelligent child. Became Dux of his school and went onto high school with great expectations. They were all very proud of him.

There was talk of forensic science – maybe police work, criminology and so on. He certainly had the ability, but in the end he left school with no clear idea of where he was headed. He had achieved an OP of 3 which was disappointing to him, but not to his family - they were proud of him. He enrolled in University but dropped out after a little more than a year – those were trying years. Everyone was amazed when he gave up University to take up an apprenticeship as a mechanic. Well! So that was a honest trade and not everyone is University material.

She moved on the hard seat, making herself a little more comfortable. What does one do with memories? Catalogue them, then box them up and tag them? No, let them run free, memories are good and they are a great inheritance. They help us to stay in contact with people we love and have loved.

Some time passed and he decided being a mechanic was not for him, having moved from that idea he moved into the world of computers. This, he decided was for him, he liked the work, so they collected all the latest technology. Craig moved out of home for a time then came back, apparently every house or flat he moved into either got sold or his friends he bunked with moved on. Very unsettling and his mother started calling him the 'Boomerang Kid' but he always came home. He had his 18th birthday party, seemed like yesterday, then came his 21st. So many friends he had, both in Australia and around the world.

He was easy to love.

There were several girlfriends, how serious, if any she did not know and she suspected his mother did not know either. But what the hell, he was a young man, probably sowing his wild oats as the saying used to be. Then he was retrenched from the job he loved, that was very sad.

He tried to learn to drive but failed the first round on a technicality. Guess he wasn't perfect after all.

It was during his employment in the Justice Department that his health gave a hic-cup and he landed in hospital. Was this the start of his problems?

They diagnosed him with depression and placed him on medication. He seemed to get better, and then he relapsed. No it wasn't cancer, maybe Crones Disease, no not that either, just a mild colitis, certainly enough to unsettle him. Then he started having trouble with his girlfriend – he had been very keen on this one, planning to ask her to marry him – a whole future ahead of him. Why? Why?

"Mum! Mum!"

A hand touched her, she opened her eyes with a start. It was really dark now and cold, she could just make out her daughter's face a few inches away looking anxious.

"Mum we were looking for you. You have been away for ages. Are you okay?"

"Yes, darling I am fine."

She looked into her daughter's sad eyes. Would she ever forget the anguish? Just a few short weeks ago, when her darling grandson, at twenty-three year's old, committed suicide, leaving his mother in so much pain, and all that loved him so dearly.

She stood up, hugged her daughter. No she would never forget. But she would learn to live with the pain and remember the happy times. They all would. She placed an arm around her daughter and knew they would get through this tragedy – time was a wonderful healer. And as they walked towards their car they turned, looked across the lake and smiled, after all they had some wonderful memories to sustain them in the passage of time.

'Don't ask the reason why – there is none.'

'Don't look to blame – there is none.'

IN MEMORY OF A GENTLE MAN

Craig Allan Springsteen

My Grandson

Remember the good times
He walked on his toes a gentle boy, Tread softly my grandson we know you are there
Though we cannot hear you, your time here was dear
                                    A grand mothers thoughts

Shh! If you are quiet, you may hear him, he walks on his toes.

THE DESERT QUEST

The Following short story was written in the main by my Grandson Craig Springsteen when he was in year 7A, had he lived I feel quite a story teller he would have been.

The Persian Desert is one of the most arid places in the world. Lucky for the Freman their ancestors learnt how to survive in the desert and passed on the skills from generation to generation. Everything was quiet in the city Tira. As normal Stilgar was teaching his fighting class, while Zar was scaling walls and practising using his invisibility ring he was given when his father died. Last of all Aziv was studying books and reading about spells and science. Suddenly there was a long howl in the distance, "The Brigands are coming" the tower guard shouted. Everyone ran to their posts and loaded there laser rifles. Silence reigned and the Fremen waited, a large shadow loomed over the city and everyone looked up to see a giant dragon flying above. The king of the Brigands, Wrath, was riding the dragon and heading straight for the tower where Aziv was. "The Howling must have been a decoy" Stilgar said. All of a sudden the dragon dropped a net on Aziv as Wrath commanded. "Don't fire!" Stilgar shouted "you might hit Lord Aziv."

The dragon screeched as it flew away.

"I've had enough of those fifthly Brigands!" Wada the head Councilman said. "I will pick the best warriors to stop those creatures once and for all. Stilgar you will be the head of the group for your strength and skill. Meek, you will join him for your craftsmanship, Scarlet for your knowledge and magic, Zar for your invisibility and stealth, finally Terin, since you are half Jackle you will go for your knowledge of the desert."

As the warriors left the city everyone prayed for them. No one knew what the desert had in store for them.

"How much longer do we have to walk till we reach the stop point?" Scarlet complained. "I'm a sorcerer not a journeyed". "Stop your complaining, witch. "Stilgar said harshly. "Look there it is now".

"I hate the desert, too many scorpions and snakes. Not to mention the heat." Meek mumbled under his breath.

"Hey, I wonder what those black dots on the horizon are." Zar questioned the group. "Well whatever it is we will check it in the morning" Scarlet insisted. "I'm so tired I can hardly move." Everyone laid out their sleeping bags and went to sleep.

"She's gone!' Zara said as he woke up each person one by one. "What, who's gone?" Stilgar said sleepily.

"Scarlet!" Zar replied

"You don't suppose she left us." Terin said

"That's impossible. Even though she didn't like the journey, she would never have left us" Zar explained.

"He's right," Stilgar said. "Her sleeping bag is still here and besides she would never let Lord Aziv down."

"Wait I put a tracking device on her, I put one on everyone before we left, we can find her like that!" Meek said excitingly. He took out a device that looked like a small computer and went over to the only tree for miles. "Accordingly to this she's right……HERE!!" He shouted in puzzlement. He looked up into the tree and saw a body that looked like Scarlet only it was skinned.

"There is only one animal in the desert that does this to its victims………GIANT NICKLEPEDES!" Terin explained

After they gave Scarlet a proper burial place, the warriors packed their belongings and left. None of them spoke a word all morning.

I'm going crazy with this heat. "Meek commented. "Ignore it" Terin said.

"That's easy for you to say, your' a Jackal "Meek said. "You used to live in the desert and

"And what "Meek," Stilgar said. The group turned around and saw Meek lying dead on the desert floor.

"Dehydration" Terin said. The Trio buried as they had done with Scarlet. They walked and walked until they reached the brigand fortress.

"Let's see" Zar whispered, "Stilgar and Terin, you will get into the fort by walking through the side battlement, I will take care of the guards. Now I think Aziv is being held in the left tower. I will get Aziv while you two clear the way to the out-look, OK? Let's go. "Zar scaled up the wall and shot the guard with a pea shooter then scaled further up the wall to the left tower. "Look out!" Stilgar shouted at Terin. But it was too late. Terin got shot in the neck and quickly bled to death. Stilgar ran up the battlements stairs and opened the roof with the control panel. Zar and Stiglar escaped with Aziv and they flew off into the sun

MY LIFE SO FAR...

By Rochelle Springsteen – while still in school.

Hi, I'm supposed to tell you about my life story…… Just a minute! Let me get myself relaxed……AHHHH! That's better! Boy, this cold water really does wonders for your skin! Oh, sorry! You don't know my name, do you? I used to be called Tabby, (silly name, Hu!) but, after the transformation, I was called Ferdy. (Still a stupid name!)

My life starts in "Fern's End", a place built just right for my mum and her mate. I was born in "Guppy's Gully", a place located in the heart of "Fern's End' Mum built a nice strong nest and settled in, while her mate (One of my Fathers,) went to find a good insect infested log to sit on.

Mum laid 3263 eggs that night. But, thanks to the guppy's, I only had 213 brothers and sisters I won't tell you all their names, but I'll tell you a few: Kiren, Kathy, Tilly, Taffy, Morris, Tommis, Tilly, Billy, Lesley and Lausen . Why I was called "Tabby", I don't know! (I guess Mum just ran out of names! Hee! Hee!).

Well, anyway, I was called Tabby. (When I finally hatched!) Mum said that I had an unusually short tail. But being what I am, she loved me just the same as my brothers and sisters. To start off with, as everyone does in "Guppy's Gully" I was small and short. I looked forward to the day when I would become a Bull.

My first day at swimming school was the pits!!

Everyone called me shortie. (This was my nickname, although I didn't know it yet.) At swimming school Mrs Croak, our teacher, taught us many things; How to avoid creatures that might eat us such as the terrible toads, (who were invading and taking over "Guppy's Gully" slowly but surely!) She taught us how to stay out of the way of larger, more fiercesom Bulls, and of course she taught us how to swim. My best friend Leggs, (so called because of his early back legs) told me about what it would be like to travel through the stages from little "Shorttie" to " Big Bull!".

Well, in the past three weeks, my tail has lengthened (as has my Nickname!) to three times its original length. Now my nickname is "Tailly"' (You may have guessed why!) Soon (In about three days,) I'll be seeing my back legs popping out from behind. But now, I am off to another day of swimming school.

These three days passed quickly. Now, my Nickname's Leggs (Because of my new back legs.) The next few days of my life were boring! So I'll just skip to the part where I get both legs and a shorter tail. It's amazing my tail starts out short, gets longer, then gets real short again!! It is so confusing! Well that just about covers my life story So Far!!

Hold on a minute!! Don't go yet! I said "Just about " I soon began to lose my "Tabby" tail . My mum spoke to me: "Tabby" really doesn't suit you now, my scaly one! It's time to change your name" So mum and her mate decided on " Ferdy" Yes!! They cried. Yes! Ferdy Frog! Our Handsome Bull!! So that is how I got my name. Well I'm getting hungry, so I'd better be going! GOOD BYE!!

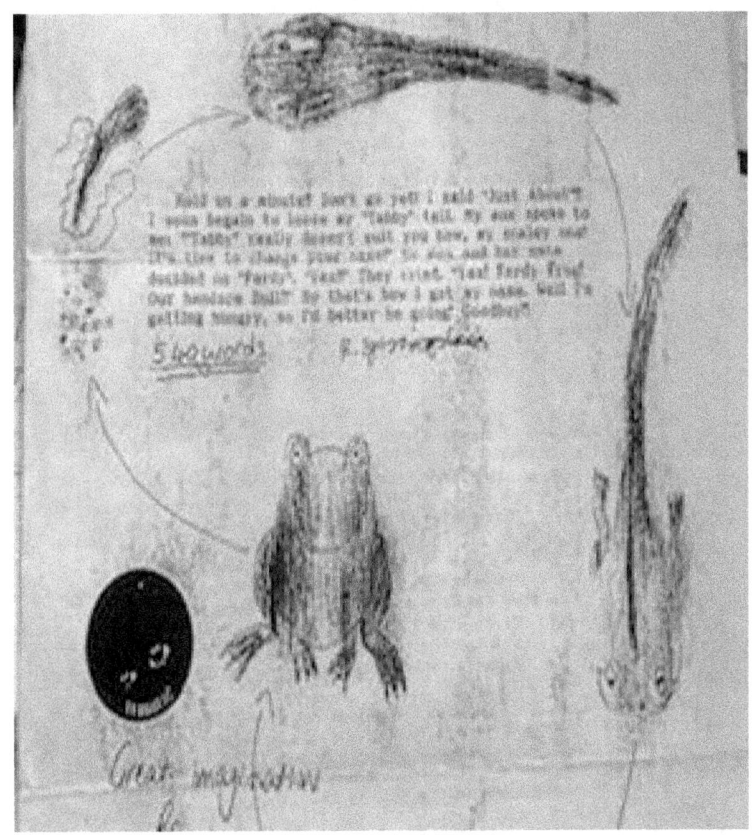

ABOUT THE AUTHOR

Judi Waller was born in Charing Cross London, England in 1935 and lived in Middlesex up to the start of World War two, (1939).

Judi and her sister Ann were sent to a convent run by Nuns for parts of the war term (prior to the breakout of the war this convent was an orphanage), but at the onset of war with Germany the doors were open to the children left isolated as their parents went to fight.

After the War, Judi moved to Falmouth in Cornwall, South England. In 1949 she immigrated to Australia with her parents, sister and brother.

Judi has worked in several jobs in Australia and PNG. After she which attained a real estate license and worked through to owning her own Real Estate Property business in Canberra ACT.

Judi completed a company Directors certificate course through the University of New England in Armadale N.S.W. At that time Judi was one of the few females to complete a Company Directors course.

One of the many things Judi has wanted to do was to write. Finally, having retired, Judi now has the time to fulfil that dream of writing short stories, her life experiences and is part way through her novel.

This anthology: The Tales End, is Judi's first book.

www.ingramcontent.com/pod-product-compliance
Lightning Source LLC
Chambersburg PA
CBHW072014290426
44109CB00018B/2239